I0792017

Strengthening the Mid-section

Professional relationship between supervisor & counselor

Dr. B.G. Nash

Forward

This work is both informative, motivationally intended and a bit of self-help. Although the primary intent of this work is to bring attention to the midsection concerning mental health and substance use organizations and facilities, the author thought it fit or appropriate to interject some elements of self-improvement for both personal and professional health care workers. The author has spent years working with health care first responders and has witnessed firsthand the stress and deep emotions they all have in taking care of the people that hold a special place in our hearts. This work places an emphasis on the relationship between supervisor and counselor because in this profession our front-line worker needs all the support we can offer. The author offers some support in this work both as a special thanks and deep appreciation of the work you all do and being the person, you all are.

Thank you,

Dr. B. G. Nash Sr. Ph. D. Th. D. LL.D. CASAC – Master Forensic Psychology

In my first work, I introduced the results of my research on transformational and transactional leadership in mental health and substance use organizations and institutes. Although the research showed that transformational leadership is favored among counselors and supervisors, there is still much information as to how these two leadership skills/styles work in the field of public and private service. If transactional leadership is the foundation of all leadership as said by Bass (1985), then when do the transformational skills/styles take effect with counselors? In this work, I describe the parts of the chain of command to give an overview of how this connection changes its mode of operation and yet never separates. Every organization realizes that keeping up with a fast-paced society driven by technology requires a consistent watch over this connection.

Nonetheless, in the field of mental health and individuals diagnosed with an addiction, providing a fast-paced service is not consistent with helping people to recover and become the individuals they hope to become. In this work, the description of this connection will include positions beginning with the authority, the midsection, and at the end of this spectrum of the client/patient. Each position is given proper attention and credit toward efforts in adjusting to policy and procedures relating to the progress and personal success of all frontline workers in the field of mental health and addictions service. This work is intended to promote views of how organizations and institutes function, and to give the reader some insight in to how the chain of command functions, while in some cases, struggling to remain competitive.

The Authority

This position requires the individual to have the experience and personal and business insights about the overall function of the organization/institute, especially as it relates to following local and state requirements. This position in the chain of command is strictly transactional because leadership must not only keep up with the changing laws but adjust spending and all other costs to provide this public service. Most recognize this position as CEO, president, or a vice president, who makes every effort to keep the doors open for individuals needing aid and those who want to serve them.

This position can be viewed at certain points as being fluid due to ever-changing laws. Yet in the same instance, it can appear rigid, distant, and uncaring. This transactional leadership position is given to directors of programs in which he or she is required to run the program according to federal and state laws. As a result, many other important responsibilities come with this position. Nevertheless, this work is intended to explain the ebb and flow of diverse institutions within the field of mental health and substance use and leadership skill/styles.

The authority figure is responsible for organizing and implementing a concrete foundation to support the legal aspect of the organization. Of course, discussing all those responsibilities is more than what can be explained in this work. It also moves away

 DR. B.G. NASH

from the focus of this work, which is strengthening the midsection in the chain of command. Still, the authority is the main link in this chain and must be transactionally connected to the legal aspect involving the institution's vision and mission statement. The mission and vision statements give the licensing agency, the public, and potential employees insight into what the institution stands for and how the future of the organization is viewed. Today, information is at the fingertips of many individuals researching available services for loved ones. They also include other licensed individuals involved within the foundation, such as social workers, mental health professionals, counselors, nurses, and other medical personnel. This gives the organization the ability to supply quality services and provide transparent services to the public and potential employees. Much like my first work, many aspects were intentionally left for a conversation, hopefully with minds searching for originality, insight, and creativity because this field must keep up with the progress of society and the information that is available to everyone. If there is one thing the field of mental health and substance use must learn, it is to be flexible in its learning process, employee education, updated training plans, and the understanding of how to engage with its employees and clients/patients. Although most directors are directly involved with employee-client engagement, they are not around to see how the training made an impact on employees unless there is visible improvement shown in the use of documentation and/or reports. Of course, the converse is also true. Lack of improvement or even a negative trend would indicate its ineffectiveness.

This is not to imply that the director or administrator should be careless toward its employees. They are required to perform in their leadership capacity as part

 DR. B.G. NASH

of the employment description. Remember, this part of leadership is transactional, ensuring that the training is run properly and effectively. From an administrative position, job training is as important as the organizing authority figure because training works in conjunction with the organization's transparency image. The public needs to know if the places they are counting on to care for loved ones are capable of performing such a job. What are the procedures? What will my loved one learn during this process? Those are just two of the questions leadership must be prepared to answer in compliance with the state regulations that govern how the organization adheres to its policies.

The Midsection

Now we come to the section the author believes every organization should have, a strong midsection. Think about an individual who visits the local gym for a good workout. The individual is concerned about that sagging stomach and feels the workout would benefit if the focus was on his or her midsection. (See where I am going with this?). After focusing on the midsection for a couple weeks, the individual notices that not only are there some improvements in the midsection, the arms, shoulders, and thighs are also getting a little better! The author used this metaphor just to illustrate the fact that when the midsection gets stronger, the extremities benefit. This politely relates to the relationship between the supervisor and the counselor, which is, in the author's opinion, the midsection of the organization or institution.

In most organizations, an overview of the clinical supervisor would find that they spend some of their time working to ensure reports are completed, program services are continuing, and help to ensure the safety of the counselor and clients or patients. Supervisors are also concerned with compliance issues, payroll, and attendance. But above all else, they are concerned with weekly supervisions of counselors to ensure counselors can work effectively and within compliance protocols. Although supervisors are considered more in line with administrators, they are also in direct line with counselors through client behavioral reports, progress reports, and legal matters. The supervisor's job is to support counselors in their roles as health-care providers.

Supervisor-counselor meetings are more than just to assess progress. Counselors are people with feelings interested in helping individuals recover. Supervisors can help counselors after they complete training leading to credentialed alcohol and substance abuse certification (CASAC or CASAC-Trainee) and those still attending educational institutions.

As we take a closer look at the relationship between these two employees, we begin to understand how important the midsection is. Supervisors are people with personal lives as well as counselors. They are at a level between higher positions and the counselors. That makes this position very difficult at times. Supervisors can be viewed as translators because in some cases, they have transactional information relating to counselors and must be aware of how this information is to be relayed.

Unlike professions in which an immediate supervisor may ask an employee to perform a task and wait for the results, in the field of mental health and substance abuse, when the supervisor asks a counselor to complete a task, he or she must ensure the counselor is comfortable and capable of implementing this task. Why? Because every decision made is for the benefit of the client and must be considered carefully. Such tasks include treatment planning, seminars, and individual therapy sessions. The curriculum must be evidence-based, and the individual sessions approved by the clinical supervisor and the organizational leadership.

Let us take a deeper look at the counselor position. Most counselors, as previously mentioned, attend educational institutes for outside support. This is not to

 DR. B.G. NASH

say that they are not prepared to serve this population. Rather, they are making every effort to ensure they have the confidence and education to perform daily job tasks. Unlike licensed social workers and other licensed employees, who may have a life-work balance in which personal life and work are compartmentalized, most counselors have three elements to address: work, personal life, and continuing their educational courses. Keeping this type of life balance takes much mental and physical energy. It also requires continuous support from the supervisor, which is the beginning of the transactional leadership relationship between supervisor and counselor.

Supervisors must be aware of the language they use when supporting counselors because they are not clients or patients. They are professionals and important parts of the team. The transactional relationship begins with the supervisor asking the counselor, for example, "What did you learn about yourself after completing a seminar? Is there anything that would help you in understanding the purpose of what you do for a living?" What the supervisor is trying to do is to lay a foundation of what the counselor personally believes, and how the counselor processes this information. This give-and-take conversation may allow the counselor to examine his or her thought process to make sense of what he or she is doing on and off the job. Let us say that the counselor did a great job completing a particular task. The supervisor may ask the counselor to explain how he or she was able to produce a great outcome. As the counselor explains the situation, the supervisor is contemplating a growth method relating to the work the counselor just completed.

The give-and-take process occurs when the supervisor takes the information and asks the counselor

   DR. B.G. NASH

to perform a similar task but at a higher level. For example, the counselor does a good job conducting seminars. The next level may be a family meeting with the client and his or her family members. This builds levels on top of levels, which allows the counselor to see the progress firsthand.

We must remember that this is a conversation between two professionals—supervisor and counselor—and the implementation of the conversation is grammatically important. Transactional leadership builds layers of progress until a solid foundation is formed. But before we take this further into the profession, let us examine the meaning, purpose, and features of transactional relationships.

Transactional leadership uses rewards and punishments to direct and motivate followers; it may be referred to as managerial leadership. This approach emphasizes the importance of supervision, structure, organization, performance, and outcome. This leadership style, however, does not directly promote growth and change. Rather, it focuses on supporting and enforcing current rules and expectations. This leadership style is effective when collaborating with employees who function well in a structured environment and those managers feel need motivation.

Okay, let's examine motivation for a moment. Transactional leadership creates motivation for a short-term goal, in which the employee is recognized when performing and knows his or her manager is always watching.

The positive aspect is that this type of leadership and structure helps everyone to experience immediate success because the employee can view the progress that's made. Transactional instructions are almost always clear and require a precise response in the implementation of a task and to eliminate confusion concerning who is in charge. Now, imagine for a moment what would happen if we turned this leadership style inside out. What would happen if all the descriptions given about transactional leadership were internal rather than external? This leadership points directly to the progress and benefits of the organization, which is simply fine. But what about the employee? What if we were to apply the description to the well-being of the employee? First, we must know the elements of transactional leadership and then perform what the author calls "organization progress vs. self-advancement."

1. Transactional leadership uses a practical approach to improving efficiency to solve problems. This limits any doubts because clear guidelines on how to continue have been set in place. A self-advancement approach occurs when the individual confronts and then learns

to understand current doubts and uncertainties within us. This is followed by the creation of clear guidelines that help the individual to reach short-term goals for self-advancement.

2. Transactional leaders are good at following routine structured tasks using linear thinking. This type of thinking is a straight-line approach without any deviations. The advantage of this approach is that it creates stability and is grounded and sustainable. A self-advancement approach example is to imagine walking on a tightrope. You must develop a sense of balance. To sustain a balance is to make the tightrope the same imaginable length as your short-term goal. This allows the individual to learn how to balance everyday situations.

3. Transactional leaders have certain expectations and guidelines to lead their employees smoothly.

 DR. B.G. NASH

This is important because when one team member steps out of the guidelines, it affects the team. Using a self-advancement approach allows the individual to set self-guidelines that are important for mental and physical health. These self-guidelines must be reachable, attainable, and above all, simple.

4. Transactional leaders are successful when goals are clearly defined and easily measured. Transactional leaders depend on this measurement because they are rewarded in return. In other words, the more productive and successful the employee is, the more confident the transactional leader becomes. A self-advancement approach to this measurement is based on the individual's self-honesty within a certain measure. Self-honesty is measured by examining every decision made during the

day about oneself while in the presence of an adversity to which we are all subjected.

5. Transactional leaders are resistant to change because it takes them out of their comfort zones. Transactional leaders depend on situations to remain the same, orderly and consistent. A self-advancement approach to this point of reference is, of course, self-discipline in ascertaining the best life balance measurement for them. Most individuals become rigid and hard toward themselves, which may lead to self-doubt.

These transactional leadership styles are related to a profession outside mental health and substance use organizations—including insurance companies, travel agencies, sales, and factory industries—most companies depend on this type of leadership because of structure-driven methods. Nonetheless, in mental health and substance use organizations, there are programs in which the counselor sees the client/patient every day. In some cases, all night! This is not a profession where we serve and forget.

We must be supportive in every meeting to ensure the clients/patients succeed in their goals. If supervisors implement self-advancement methods, the counselor feels empowered and develops confidence. And when this occurs, both the organization and the individual grow. Each self-advancement method creates a transactional foundation when they are built upon each other, and ultimately, the transformational attribute develops. But before we get to the transformational attributes, the author would like to point out that there is a gray area between transactional and transformational leadership attributes.

The author calls this gray area "transformactional." This is the period when the individual determines if he or she is ready to build on the transactional foundation. If I may, I would like to offer a metaphor. "The foundation is stable and ready to build on it." If someone said that, what would this look like? If the foundations taken from the previously mentioned self-advancement process, you would have to wonder, *Would I become a leader? A good follower? Or someone who creates through originality?* This gray area can be viewed as neutrality and impartiality, a place where the individual would experience a sense of calm and order. It is a place where the individual can take a step back and assess the situation giving a sense of perspective, a particular way of viewing things that depends on one's experience and personality. This approach to the transformactional is not considered a leadership style or skill, but it may allow the individual to examine how much is achieved through the evaluation of the self-advancement steps. Symbolically, it is intellect and compromise negotiating measurement between black and white.

This gray area may be perceived as potential, which could be understood as "currently unrealized ability," and "possibilities" is the capability of existing or happening or being true. This is important because the individual is given the chance to build on the self-advancement steps to create a stronger foundation. Building a solid professional foundation is not an easy task today. There are many aspects contained in one position, which is why this relationship is an integral part of this profession. Most individuals come into this field to help others and need support to become the best professionals possible. Of course, they want to build on their personal lives as well.

Now that we have an idea of how to start building a personal and professional foundation, let's examine transformational leadership.

Unlike transactional leadership, transformational leadership is more authoritative, a leading-by-example type of leadership. This guidance is inspirational, which influences workers to achieve amazing and startling results that allow workers autonomy over certain tasks and the ability to make decisions. They find diverse methods to achieving goals, can motivate groups, boost morale, raise well-being through positive rapport, and are good at conflict resolution. The characteristics of transformational leadership complement self-advancement steps because this is what the individual will build upon. In other words, transactional leadership supplies the foundation, and transformational leadership is what is built upon it!

1. *Idealized Influence (II)*: This leadership is considered a role model for workers as it exemplifies worker characteristics. They

lead by supplying positive examples. This is a supporting example of the first self-advancement statement.

2. *Inspirational Motivation (IM)*: Transformational leadership motivates by providing a clear vision and communicating this vision to workers. And when conjoined with idealized influence, it represents the leader and workers' productivity.

3. *Individualized Consideration (IC)*: Transformational leaders show interest in their workers' emotions. This is very important because our frontline counselors are subject to many situations that may trigger emotional responses. Transformational leaders give individuals the attention they need for reinforcement. This should be mentioned during supervision meetings as it contributes to the development of the self-advancement steps.

4. *Intellectual Stimulation (IS)*: This reinforces the foundation through positive encouragement, creativity, becoming innovative, asking questions concerning tasks, and understanding purpose and instruction.

The self-advancement steps illustrate how the counselor may become more effective in both professional and personal areas of life. But there is a main topic that must be considered. These attributes concerning transactional, transformactional, and transformational are explained from an external perspective. This perspective would serve the reader well when implemented internally.

As we dig deeper into the attributes, we can begin to understand that what makes organizations, companies, and institutions successful may allow counselors and supervisors to become personally and professionally successful. Transformational leaders believe they can tap into the potential of others to reach goals. If this holds true, an individual could access this potential as well (unrealized ability). Furthermore, if transactional leaders believe they can build organizational foundations, so can we! Transformational leaders do not rely on the power given to them through organizational authority, but they depend on the ability to visualize and motivate others to see this vision (Northouse, 2016).

To fully understand and grasp the uniqueness of these leadership styles/types, the individual must be mindful of the purpose: to run a company! Nevertheless, if these attributes were incorporated within the supervisor and counselor relationship, not only would this bring efficient productivity, it would enhance the lives of both parties! It is about self-development in leadership qualities that make a lasting impression. However, transactional leadership gives the individual an understanding of what needs to be changed, transformactional allows us to examine and evaluate, and transformational brings the work to the surface.

There are other reasons this relationship is important—burnout. This has been defined as a complex psychological syndrome that manifests in response to prolonged exposure to chronic stressors (Maslach, Schaufeli, & Leiter, 2001). This is commonly recognized in occupations such as health care, teaching, law enforcement, social services, and particularly in behavioral health-care workers. The bottom line is that most professions today, regardless of the market, find themselves trying to do more with less (Lewis, 2008). This is where the relationship between supervisor and counselor matters.

Leadership entails being a positive influence, a role model whom one looks up to for inspiration and direction They supply vision and inspiration and effectively steer change and encourage everyone who has abilities to complete tasks. This concept of empowering everyone to be a leader is consistent with the notion of encouragement in rehabilitation counseling as it correlates to supporting individuals with disabilities to become self-governing. All rehabilitation counselors must begin to view themselves as leaders in the profession. More important, as leaders who can transform the profession. This statement alludes to the self-advancement steps during the transactional phase, which builds the foundation. And then allowing the counselor to contemplate the gray area (transformactional) while learning how to create a situational balance by examining areas of doubt, distractions, and unrealized abilities (unrealized potential). Finally, advancing to transformational phase.

This type of transformational leadership is successful when rehabilitation counselors and supervisors incorporate a set of harmonizing skills between supervisor and counselor. The skills are intercultural ability and looking forward to the future. "Creating companies learning people, employing a complete structure for planning change, engaging in data-driven decision making and critical thinking" (Lewis, Graham, & Quamar, 2014). Intercultural competency includes social and personal awareness and control over one's personal biases. "This personal control limit the potential negative impact in work with others while striving to enhance the therapeutic alliance through supporting commonalities" (Lewis et al., 2014).

This is an illustration of forward-thinking that is not limited to organizational growth but to developing, supporting, and above all, strengthening the relationship between supervisor and counselor. Foreseeing the future involves an inclination to not be complacent with past success. "Learning anew in situations as needed, looking for innovation on the edge of the profession where other professions have influence, and routinely posing questions that exceed today's standard practice and venture into a realm of innovation" (Barker, 1993).

Individuals working in rehabilitation programs often fall into repetitious work habits like a structure that remains the same each day. Nonetheless, becoming creative within the organization's policies requires new ideas and innovations to keep up with ever-changing public needs. "Making organizations learning entities entails striving to think ahead of crises and routinely engaging in systems thinking, collective visioning, team learning, and personal mastery" (Senge, 1990).

This "personal mastery" brings us back to the self-advancement steps. Developing the vision to think ahead of a crisis requires the internal development of self, building and supporting confidence to respond proactively. "Systematically planning for change involves proactively targeting change tactics at the individual, interpersonal, organizational, community and policy levels (as per the Social Ecological model" (McLeroy, Bibeau, Steckler, & Glanz, 1988). "Critical thinking requires self-development and analytic discerning perception that regularly questions the purpose, context, expectations, persuasive tactics, and evidence in all communication situations" (Lewis et al., 2014). These statements point to both the individual and the organizational frameworks, growth, and productivity.

"The adoption of these skills in conjunction with transformational leadership the Rehabilitation

Counselors would not only become experts in their field but proficient in cultural situations" (Lewis et al., 2014). Until now, this work has given the reader an overview of the system, self-improvement, and the motivation to change public beliefs and stigmas. In this work, the author emphasized how strengthening the midsection of this field would possibly—capability of existing or happening or being true—reinforce the current structure and bring workplace innovations. Still, employees are people! We are all capable of making mistakes that may not be in line with the organization's policies, rules, and/or regulations and could be perceived as a learning process of balanced growth.

This work focuses on the relationship between supervisor and counselor development toward a more positive work relationship and developing a positive personal lifestyle through self-advancement. But would this relationship behavior hold to this point? Although this work illustrates the order of the chain of command—the authority figure, the midsection (supervisor and counselor), and the client/patient—there must be guidelines that help keep this chain connected. In other words, organizational ethics! In 1994, due to the change in accreditation standards, the medical field gained social attention (Ellis & MacDonald, 2002). This is defined as, "the study and practice of the ethical behavior of healthcare organizations," the intentional use of values to guide the decisions of a system. Kaptien and Wempe (1998) suggested that "an organizational code cannot be written down and that employees should become immersed in the environment and observe the behaviors of other employee's behavior patterns."

If this is the case, the supervisor and counselor would benefit by examining the transformactional section of this work, which illustrates the gray area that is elusive in most cases. The observation of an employee's patterns, suggested by Kaptien and Wempe (1998), may show the true organizational ethical code. Would this cause some distractions within the relationship between the supervisor and counselor? Or should this be considered during weekly supervision, with a focus on how to work in conjunction with employee observation? Organizational codes involve the agency as a whole, from administrators to clinicians, to prove professional status (Remley & Herlihy, 2005). This transactional statement also includes the fact that,

> It is common in a rehabilitation and substance abuse facility to find psychologist, social workers, rehabilitation counselors with no formal training collaborating with each other ... This means that any counselor could

hold multiple affiliations which gave rise to numerous ethical codes governing any one agency that may conflict, provide vague answers to common issues. (Remley & Herlihy, 2005)

In the alcohol and other drug abuse (AODA) field, which does not make any mention of mental health, it is noted that multiple supervisory relationships occur more often than in mental health and substance use organizations. These multiple relationships between supervisor and counselor are based on religion, social, culture, business, or sex (Ray, 2006). It is helpful for the supervisor and counselor relationship to know that within the counseling field, there are no clear and concrete definitions of supervision. It may be interpreted in multiple ways (Tromski-Klingshirm, 2006).

Earlier in this work, the author described transactional leadership as "being clear and precise,"

 DR. B.G. NASH

but this statement points to the definition, not the leadership skill/style itself. However, a general definition is understood as "critical, watching and directing" (*Merriam-Webster's Online Dictionary*, n.d.). The mention of multiple relationships and the definition of supervisor are mentioned here because the more the counselor knows about the peripheral view, the more this gray area is understood (transformactional).

The definition of a supervisor includes anyone in an educational setting who may have some influence on the assessment of the trainee, particularly in a medical residency program. Thus, in the field of AODA counseling, while including aspects of the medical field, a supervisor is to be more than simply a silent observer, "but also an educator, trainer, evaluator, and potentially (unrealized ability) a mentor to ensure professionals allowed to enter the field have the appropriate skills and competencies" (Recupero,

Cooney, Rayner, Heri, and Price, 2005). This could be viewed as transactional leadership in which the foundational needs are met and illustrated by the supervisor, who is directed and governed by the code of ethics.

As the author said earlier in this work, the transactional, transformactional, and transformational relationship and self-advancement steps can be achieved within the policies and codes of ethics. However, the transformactional area should be fully understood because, in mental health and substance use organizations, the authority figures must support a certain order within the organization. West, Mustaine, and Wyrick (1999), "found that 21 out of 34 states surveyed made no reference to a requirement for clinical supervision, or if a reference was made, no qualification requirement for supervisors was stated."

However, it was reported that a new supervisor would highly depend on the experience of other supervisors to get a concrete example of an acceptable function of the practice (Powell & Brodsky, 2004). This is important because, "the provision of clinical supervision is central to the development of new and experienced rehabilitation counselors" (Herbert & Ward, 1989; Maki & Delworth, 1995). Supervision is believed to have positive effects on supervisee counseling skills and other professional development processes (Schultz, 2007; Steward, 1998). It is also stated that "despite the unrealized ability (potential) benefits of supervision, we as clinical supervisors may not be as intentional in promoting development as we could be" (Bernard & Goodyear, 2009). This implies that supervision is given as needed, which results in irregular meetings of short duration between counselor and supervisor.

This short duration may be comprised of problem-solving and instructing counselors on corrective record-keeping. Very little is provided in the way of practice and/or internship, which results in an inconsistent, passive approach (Herbert & Trusty, 2006; Schultz et al., 2002). As stated earlier, supervisors are tasked with many other obligations that prove to be multifaceted, quite complex, and employ different styles of supervision depending on the needs of the supervisee (Friedlander & Ward, 1984). "This neglect has been shown to have a negative impact on the rehabilitation counselor" (Herbert & Trusty, 2006). Regardless of the potential of supervision in the development of counseling skills and professional identity, very little has been studied to understand the long-standing deficiencies or flaws in clinical supervision.

However, using the combination of self-efficacy and outcome expectancies may provide a plausible but limited explanation for the lack of proactive and consistent supervision in rehabilitation counseling. Psychologist Albert Bandura has defined self-efficacy as people's beliefs in their abilities to exert self-control over their performances and over events that affect their lives. One's sense of self-efficacy can provide the foundation for motivation, well-being, and personal achievement. People's beliefs in their efficacy are developed by four main sources of influence: mastery experiences, explicit experiences, social encouragement, and emotional states. "High self-efficacy has been linked with numerous benefits to daily life, such as resilience to adversity and stress, healthy lifestyle habits, improved employees' performance, and educational achievement" (Lopez-Garrido 2020). Nonetheless, the literature places a focus primarily on the supervisee and not the relationship between supervisor and counselor.

When we illuminate the other party—the supervisor—we see a one-sided relationship in which the supervisor must develop the abovementioned professional and personal skills based on their life and professional experiences. It is safe to assume that without the relationship between the supervisor and counselor, the midsection may not gain the momentum to maintain the modality of the chain of command. Remember: The chain of command only changes its mode to remain flexible but retains the strength and resilience of the organization. Although self-efficacy is built on the foundational principles, cognitive processes, mediate behaviors, and our cognitions are shaped by the mastery experiences that result from successful task performance (Bandura, 1977; Strauser, 1995). This is in line with the self-advancement steps. But we must take into consideration, "What if both parties were to develop this type of self-mastery?"

 DR. B.G. NASH

This implies that self-efficacy is domain—immediate environment—and task-specific—what must be accomplished in this environment—where the individual may perform high in some tasks and lower in other tasks (Bandura, 1977; Strauser, 1995). We recall the three methods of understanding leadership—transactional (foundation), transformactional (gray area), and transformational (building on the previous two leadership skills/styles). The above statement is transactional, which begins the foundational steps required to build the relationship between supervisor and counselor. "Complementary to the construct of self-efficacy, outcome expectancies are defined as a person's estimate that given a behavior will lead to certain outcomes" (Bandura, 1977, p. 193). Is this the gray area mentioned? Transformactional thinking examines the peripheral, potential (unrealized ability), and measurement between black and white, what is immediately realized and what is not immediately realized.

In this outcome expectancy, the clinical supervisor believes supervision will increase counselor competence in counseling skills such as closing a case and implementing successful group and individual sessions, by which the counselor will gain administrative recognition. "The knowledge and skills of a clinical supervisor are distinct from the knowledge and skills of a rehabilitation counselor" (Thielsen & Leahy, 2001). This suggests that training in supervisory approaches to organizational content may lead to effective supervision for the rehabilitation counselor.

As mentioned earlier in this work, transactional leadership is possible (realized ability) when considering organizational requirements. We would ask, "Should the clinical supervisor require some psychology training to provide a positive approach to transactional leadership for the rehabilitation counselor? The author is inclined to say yes because along with professional experience, the clinical supervisor must also develop self-awareness and the ability to focus on what the rehabilitation counselor needs to become successful.

Many studies have been conducted on counselor self-efficacy, which focused primarily on the level of self-efficacy—the ability to believe a task or goal can be achieved—counselor development, training, and levels of anxiety (Tang et al., 2004). However, research shows a positive relationship between counselor self-efficacy and the alliance with a clinical supervisor, but it was not extended to include the self-efficacy of the clinical supervisor. As we can clearly understand, it takes much effort in the learning process for the midsection to maintain stability, integrity, self-development, and self-advancement for the chain of command to remain resilient and intact. Nevertheless, this work is dedicated to internal self-advancement and the relationship between supervisor and counselor. "Clinical supervision is important to the profession and practice in health sciences and human services which is indisputable and have been increasingly recognized as a critical element in training and preparation" (Jones, 2006).

Professional programs like social work, family medicine, rehabilitation counseling, physical therapy, clinical psychology, alcohol and drug dependency, and nursing require direct, one-on-one supervision to enhance their professional skills. In fact, "the supervisory relationship plays a more important role than the actual techniques or methods used to ensure effective supervision" (Inman et al., 2014; Kilminster & Jolly, 2000). Okay, at this point, the reader should recognize we are making a full circle. This fact

  DR. B.G. NASH

reinforces the main scope of this work because if supervision is to be more important than techniques and methods, building a transactional foundation makes perfect sense when it is learned internally. What the author has witnessed in this field is that people come to help others simply because helping others is priceless. Nevertheless, we must learn to help ourselves first!

As discussed earlier, transactional leadership is based on exchanges between the leader and the follower in meeting specific goals (Aarons, 2006). This is, of course, an external statement leaning toward the organization's goals because transactional leadership is important to facilitating stability in the organization. In conjunction with the individual, a realistic personal foundational goal must be established based on transactional attributes, like minimizing personal biases and learning to understand different cultures.

This could be considered an internal give-and-take exchange that not only enhances the counselor but also helps him or her become a more informative person. "This is a very important issue because limited time is devoted to supervision in general and the counselor would have to depend on experience or training" (Herbert & Trusty, 2006).

> Transformational leadership focuses on values and beliefs and seeks to inspire followers to join in a shared vision by empowering followers and developing individual potential. (Lowder, 2009; Tyssen et al., 2014)

> One of the primary functions of supervisors is to raise the underlying motivational levels of their supervisees by emphasizing values and the way in

 DR. B.G. NASH

which values help to achieve the goals of the agency. (Aarons, 2006)

Developing unrealized ability? Raise underlying motivational levels? This may be directed toward the personal and professional growth of the counselor. But from an administrative point of view, it is for the success of the agency. Don't take a negative perception with this statement. If the individual can learn through supervision meetings, unrealized abilities can then possibly become realized abilities and find the underlying motivations!

Furthermore, if the supervisor's primary function is developing counselor potential (unrealized ability), then should the supervisor develop the same? In other words, how would the clinical supervisor guide the counselor in developing potential unless the former has experienced his or her own development? Moreover, raise motivational levels? The author suggests that a relationship between supervisor and counselor becomes one of professional and personal development sharing the self-advancement steps. What we must realize is that motivation and potential are internal energies that may be within the described gray area. Supervisors may motivate counselors with a transactional benefit by explaining the rewards of helping others and, in turn, getting noticed by administrators and achieving a feeling of self-accomplishment. But how much of this does the counselor get to personally master? Furthermore, what does the supervisor take away as far as personal and professional mastery? We must ask ourselves, "What will happen if this modality in the chain further weakens?"

During supervision sessions, in this author's professional opinion, just ask basic questions, such as whether they like the working environment, other workers, and how they feel about being employed in this field. Questions should reflect motivational elements. What moves them to do this work and why? However, unless the clinical supervisor has the personal experience of exploring his or her internal motivations, how would the supervisor interpret the answers?

Here is one statement to understand: This is a conversation between two professionals learning how to improve, not only a work ethic, but build a foundation leading to personal and professional originality. When one develops an original theory, internal motivation is likely to become a possibility, realized ability. This statement resonates through this work because of its importance: The primary function of supervision is to increase the competency of counselors at *all* levels (Maki & Delworth, 1995; Tarvydas, 1995).

While we are on the topic of the supervisor and counselor relationship, multicultural counseling should be considered. There are people of many cultures coming into the field of mental health and substance use (Matrone & Leahy, 2005; Middleton et al., 2000; Smart & Smart, 1997; Wheaton & Granello, 1998). Supervisors and counselors need to fully appreciate and understand individuals from different cultural backgrounds. This emphasizes learning how to apply culturally appropriate techniques (Diller, 2004). Administrators, supervisors, and counselors must be motivated, prepared, and educated about diversity issues (Harley, Mpofu, & Ford, 2005). This issue is not limited to counselor and client, but counselor and supervisor, which begins with a framework defined by Sue et al. (1982).

The framework is comprised of three elements: counselor awareness of personal assumptions, values, and biases; understanding worldviews; and the development of appropriate intervention, strategies, and techniques from a professional perspective. The communication between supervisor and counselor would discuss counselor beliefs and attitudes, knowledge, and skills (Sue et al., 1982). "With the increase of interactions between differing cultural groups it becomes less and less of an option for supervisors to ignore cultural difference and their impact on performance and performance appraisals" (Ivey & Ivey, 2003). Rehabilitation administrators with multicultural competencies and working knowledge of multicultural-appropriate performance appraisals will be able to better assess the work performance of culturally different supervisees and counselors. Because the field is culturally changing, with counselors and supervisors from different cultural backgrounds coming into the field, the more informative administrators must be professional and personable. This is the most important issue of this work, understanding cultures and diverse backgrounds of the clinical supervisor, counselor, and the appropriate approach to the clinical function.

"Cultural humility is the practice of respecting and accepting different cultural identities" (Hook et al., 2013). "It is a life-long process of self-reflection and contemplation" (Tervalon & Murry-Garcia, 1998). When we read these two statements, it gives a more vivid perspective to the understanding of transactional, transformactional, and transformational self-advancement steps. Educators and supervisors should encourage this method in the counselor training and supervision sessions, which would illustrate the importance of promoting self-reflection and self-privilege, and recognizing personal and professional biases. Self-reflection can be described as one looking inward to honestly examine how one views the world and how it works. The counselor and supervisor would

 DR. B.G. NASH

become aware of self-privilege and biases through self-reflection as this process is a vital part of clinical training.

"Clients have reported that a strong therapeutic alliance leads to a success counseling experiences" (Davis et al., 2016). This statement is very important because it points not only to the relationship between counselor and client but to the relationship between supervisor and counselor. When this alliance is strong, repairing ruptures in the relationship becomes a team effort! The development of the self-advancement steps allows the counselor to evolve in his or her cultural identity, in which cultural humility increases the importance of the counselor and supervisor relationship as part of the clinical learning process. "Cultural humility is a lifelong learning process of self-reflection and critique" (Tervalon & Murry-Garcia, 1998). This implies that learning and practicing self-evaluation are the foundational transactional self-advancement steps and the stability leading to success.

The reader must keep in mind that cultural humility is not limited to the counselor and client but also the supervisor and counselor. As an example, suppose the clinical supervisor's culture is different from the counselor's. Would there be an effort in understanding humility within the professional relationship? In this author's professional experience, there are more diverse cultures entering the field of mental health and substance abuse because of public and social concerns about addictions. The cultural differences between supervisor and counselor should be as diverse as the community it serves. There are Hispanic, African American, and Caucasian counselors and supervisors, just to mention a few.

But let us not forget that lesbian, gay, bisexual, transgender, queer, and other sexually and gender-diverse (LGBTQ+) youth and adults are more likely to experience mental health symptomology and meet the criteria of a substance use or mood disorder when compared to their heterosexual and cisgender peers (Bockting et al., 2013; Bostwick et al., 2010; Lipson et al., 2019; McCabe et al., 2009; Ploderl & Tremblay, 2015). Empirical evidence shows disparities, discrimination, stigma, and bias involving this population (Argyriou et al., 2021; Hendricks & Tesia, 2012; Meyer, 2003). Most therapists/counselors are not professionally prepared to serve the LGBTQ+ population because of inaccuracy in conceptualizing sexual orientation and gender-identity-related challenges. Is not having counselors and supervisors from the same population a part of the cause? There should be more LGBTQ+ supervisors and counselors because research suggests that "LGBTQ+ clients utilize mental behavioral health care services at higher rates

than their heterosexual and cisgender counterparts"
(Dunbar et al., 2017; Platt et al., 2018). Client
satisfaction increases when there are knowledgeable,
unique services as opposed to traditional therapeutic
services (Senreich, 2009, 2010). Could this be because
the counselors and clinical supervisors developed a
solid foundation in humility and self-advancement? If
this is true, then the many other therapists/counselors
who feel ill-equipped to address the unique needs of
this population may want to take note of how this is
accomplished (Rock et al., 2010). It is about having
misconceptions about this population, which is
why cultural humility, self-advancement steps, and
understanding the gray area (motivational, unrealized
ability) are important in serving all people. If there
were more LGBTQ+ supervisors and counselors/
therapists, microaggressions and stress would lessen
(Rees et al., 2021). These microaggressions include

the assumption that sexual orientation is the cause of the problems, using cis-heteronormative language, and misconceptions concerning gender expression. Most clinicians, counselors, and therapists depend on educational development to improve the quality of services when working with LGBTQ+ populations. However, these opportunities are limited and may not be a requirement.

As we can clearly understand, there is much to do in this field as addictions spread throughout our society. Even though there are no quick fixes, there is a starting point: strengthening the midsection. Throughout this work, the author emphasized supervisors and counselors, which maintains the order of services provided. But these professionals need the support of the administration and educational organizations. A balanced relationship between these two professionals is beneficial to the organization and the clients served.

But developing a satisfactory balance in this field is not an easy task because of ever-changing caseloads, reports, and meetings. Clinical supervisors can have more than three counselors at any given time, attend meetings, check reports for accuracy, and answer to administrative leaders. Much like counselors who work with many clients while having to keep up with reports, individual sessions, and conduct group meetings. Both professionals perform tasks within the scope of their employment descriptions with little or no time to meet with each other. This is mentioned to make the point that a solid relationship is important but not impossible. For this relationship to work, self-humility, self-development, and the understanding of each leadership style/skill must be devoted to culture, background, and personal understanding. Administrators and supervisors encourage employees to support each other, and the only way this can happen is when we understand each other on a professional level. This entails not only becoming aware of personal and/or professional biases but raising the level of professionalism, which begins with the self.

Thus far, we have talked about personal responsibilities, learning about ourselves and what we as professionals bring to the table, how this relationship between clinical supervisor and counselor works if the relationship is based on self-honesty, transparent work ethics, and dedication to helping not only individuals who seek our help but also the organization. Staff and all those responsible for supporting this profession would benefit by viewing this chain and its weakest link.

Clinical supervisors would be able to offer more support through a dedicated position. It's not about illuminating any links; it is more about adjusting a single link! As it stands, clinical supervisors have the responsibility of answering to higher administrators and supervising clinical staff. Clinical supervisors should be proactive and knowledgeable concerning their counselors' daily caseloads and how they work with clients. But this is asking a lot because clinical supervisors are currently required to do other administrative duties. Until we come up with theories concerning clinical functions, shared responsibilities, and the supervisor-counselor relationship, there will always be an issue with staying in tune with the addiction epidemic, which increased during and after the pandemic.

The author makes no claim to having an absolute resolution but rather offers a theory for those who care to make changes for the betterment of our clients, staff, and administrators. This work is a brief overview of suggested theories aimed at the skills either experienced or academically acquired through our

 DR. B.G. NASH

educational system. Experienced clinicians are aware of the huge responsibilities and shortage of counselors that result in overworked personnel. And if there is anything this work brings to the table it is the choices we must make so this profession is as fulfilling as it could be.

Balance is tedious upon the apex, but it is on either side of the apex that balance matters.

Let's start a conversation!

Unrealized ability, realized ability.

Potential   possibilities

References

Argyriou, A., Goldsmith, K. A., & Rimes, K. A.
(2021). Mediators of the disparities in depression
between sexual minority and heterosexual
individuals: A systematic review. *Archives of Sexual
Behavior,* 50(3), 925–959. https://doi.org/10.1007/
s10508-020-01862-0.

Bandura, A. (1977). Self-efficacy: Toward a unifying
theory of behavioral change. *Psychological Review,*
84, 191–215.

Bandura, A. (1982). Self-efficacy mechanism in human agency. *American Psychologist, 37*(2), 122–147.

Bandura, A. (1997). *Self-Efficacy: The Exercise of Control.* (New York: W. H. Freeman.)

Barker. J. A. (1993). *Paradigms: The Business of Discovering the Future.* New York: Harper Business Publishers.

Bowers, L., Nijman, H., Simpson, A., et al. (2010). The relationship between leadership, teamwork, structure, burnout and attitude to patients on acute psychotic wards. *Social Psychiatry Epidemiology.*

Bostwick, W. B., Boyd, C. J., Hughes, T. L., & McCabe, S. E. (2010). Dimensions of sexual orientation and the prevalence of mood and anxiety disorders in the United States. *American Journal of Public*

Health, 100(3), 468–475. https://doi.org/10.2105/AJPH.2008.152942.

Bockting, W. O., Miner, M. H., Swinburne Romine, R. E., Hamilton, A., & Coleman, E. (2013). Stigma, mental health, and resilience in an online sample of the US transgender

population. *American Journal of Public Health,* 103(5), 943–951. https://doi.org/10.2105/AJPH.2013.301241.

Dunbar, M. S., Sontag-Padilla, L., Ramchand, R., Seelam, R., & Stein, B. D. (2017). Mental health service utilization among lesbian, gay, bisexual, and questioning or queer college students. *The Journal of Adolescent Health,* 61(3), 294–301. https://doi.org/10.1016/j.jadohealth.2017.03.008

Friedlander, M. L., & Ward, L. G. (1984). Development and validation of the supervisory styles inventory. *Journal of Counseling Psychology*, 31, 541–557.

Goodyear, R. K. (1998). Research and practice. Implications of the SCMCT: Observations and comments. *The Counseling Psychologist*, 26, 274–284.

Harley, D. A., Mpofu, E., & Ford, H. (2005). Tokenism and minorities in rehabilitation administration and leadership: Implications for the new millennium. *Journal of Rehabilitation Administration*, 24, 73–88.

Hendricks, M. L., & Testa, R. J. (2012). A conceptual framework for clinical work with transgender and gender nonconforming clients: An adaptation of the Minority Stress Model. *Professional Psychology, Research and Practice*, 43(5), 460–467. https://doi.org/10.1037/a0029597.

Hook, J. N., Davis, D. E., Owen, J., Worthington Jr., E. L., & Utsey, S. O. (2013). Cultural humility: Measuring openness to culturally diverse clients. *Journal of Counseling Psychology* 60(3). https://doi.org/0.1037/a0032595.

Hung-Jen Kuo, Landon, T. J., Connor, A., & Chen, R. K. (2016). Managing anxiety in clinical supervision. *Journal of Rehabilitation,* 82(3), 18–27.

Herbert, J. T., & Trusty, J. (2006). Clinical supervision practices and satisfaction within the public vocational rehabilitation program. *Rehabilitation Counseling Bulletin,* 49, 66–80.

Ivey, A. E., & Ivey, M. B. (2003). *Intentional Interviewing and Counseling: Facilitation Client Development in a Multicultural Society* (5th ed.) (Pacific Grove, CA: Brooks/Cole–Thomson Learning).

Lipson, S. K., Raifman, J., Abelson, S., & Reisner, S. L. (2019). Gender minority mental health in the U.S.: Results of a national survey on college campuses. *American Journal of Preventive Medicine*, 57(3), 293–301. https://doi.org/10.1016/j.amepre.2019.04.025.

Lopez-Garrido, G. (August 9, 2020). Self-efficacy. *Simply Psychology*. www.simplypsychology.org/self-efficacy.html.

Lewis, A. (2014). Disability disparity research in 2015 and beyond: Toward a focus on solutions. *Journal of Neuroscience and Rehabilitation*, 1(2), 1–4.

Lewis, A.N., Graham, K. M., & Quamar, A. H. (2014). Beyond discipline-based expertise: Preparing global leaders in rehabilitation. *Journal of Applied Rehabilitation Counseling*, 45(2), 26–31.

Maslach C., & Jackson S. E. (1981). The measurement of experienced burnout. *Journal of Occupational Behavior*, 2, 99–113.

Maslach, C., Schaufeli, W. B., & Leiter, M. P. (2001). Job burnout. *Annual Review of Psychology*, 52, 397–422.

McCabe, S. E., Hughes, T. L., Bostwick, W. B., West, B. T., & Boyd, C. J. (2009). Sexual orientation, substance use behaviors and substance dependence in the United States. *Addiction*, 104(8), 1333–1345. https://doi.org/ 10.1111/j.1360-0443.2009. 02596.x.

McLeroy, K. F., Bibeau, D., Steckler, A., & Glanz, K, (1988). An ecological perspective on health promotion programs. *Health Education Quarterly*, 75(4), 351–377.

Meyer, I. H. (2003). Prejudice, social stress, and mental health in lesbian, gay, and bisexual populations:

Conceptual issues and research evidence. *Psychological Bulletin, 129*(5), 674–697. https://doi.org/10.1037/0033- 2909.129.5.674.

Northouse, P. G. (2016). *Leadership: Theory and Practice.* 7th edition. (Los Angeles: Sage Publications).

Platt, L. F., Wolf, J. K., & Scheitle, C. P. (2018). Patterns of mental health care utilization among sexual orientation minority groups. *Journal of Homosexuality, 65*(2), 135–153. https://doi.org/10.1080/00918369.2017 .1311552.

Phillips, B. N., Schultz, J. C., & Thielsen, V. A. (2012). Supervisor self-efficacy, outcome expectancies, and the provision of clinical supervision in rehabilitation counseling. *Journal of Rehabilitation Administration, 36*(1), 17–25.

Plöderl, M., & Tremblay, P. (2015). Mental health of sexual minorities. A systematic review. *International Review of Psychiatry*, 27(5), 367–385. https://doi.org/10.3109/09540261.2015.1083949.

Rees, S. N., Crowe, M., & Harris, S. (2021). The lesbian, gay, bisexual and transgender communities' mental health care needs and experiences of mental health services: An integrative review of qualitative studies. *Journal of Psychiatric and Mental Health Nursing*, 28(4), 578–589. https://doi.org/10.1111/jpm.12720.

Rock, M., Carlson, T. S., & McGeorge, C. R. (2010). Does affirmative training matter? Assessing CFT students' beliefs about sexual orientation and their level of affirmative training. *Journal of Marital and Family Therapy*, 36(2), 171–184. https://doi.org/10.1111/j.1752-0606.2009.00172.x

Senge, Peter M. (1990). The fifth discipline: The art and practice of the learning organization, *The Fifth Discipline: The Art & Practice of The Learning Organization* (New York: Doubleday).

Sue, D. W., Bernier, J. E., Durran, A., Feinberg, L., Pedersen, P., Smith, E. J., & Vasquez-Nuttall, E. (1982). Position paper: Cross-cultural counseling competencies. *The Counseling Psychologist*, 10, 45–52.

Senreich, E. (2009). A comparison of perceptions, reported abstinence, and completion rates of gay, lesbian, bisexual, and heterosexual clients in substance abuse treatment. *Journal of Gay & Lesbian Mental Health*, 13(3), 145–169. https://doi.org/10.1080/19359700902870072.

Senreich, E. (2010). Differences in outcomes, completion rates, and perceptions of treatment between white, Black, and Hispanic LGBT clients in substance abuse programs. *Journal of Gay & Lesbian Mental Health*, 14(3), 176–200. https://doi.org/10.1080/19359701003784675.

Tang, M., Addison, K. D., Lasure-Bryant, D., Norman, R., O'Connell, W., & Stewart-Sicking, J. A. (2004). Factors that influence self-efficacy of counseling students: An exploratory study. *Counselor Education and Supervision*, 44(1), 70–80.

Thielsen, V. A., & Leahy, M. J. (2001). Essential knowledge and skills for effective clinical supervision in rehabilitation counseling. *Rehabilitation Counseling Bulletin*, 44, 196–208.